THE LAW, THE BROKEN JUDICIAL SYSTEM & POLICE BRUTALITY IN BARBADOS 2

Apostle Marguerite Breedy-Haynes

Rehoboth

Barbados

THE LAW ,THE BROKEN JUDICIAL SYSTEM & POLICE BRUTALITY IN BARBADOS 2

Rehoboth books may be ordered through Amazon.com and other booksellers.

Breedy-Haynes, Marguerite
The Law, The Broken Judicial System & Police Brutality In Barbados 2

ISBN-13: 9798883460387

Printed in the United States of America

Dedication

I dedicate this Booklet to Jesus Christ my Lord and
Savior who is the lover of my soul and to the precious
Holy Spirit who continues to walk with me and teaches
me all things

Contents

Introduction

God is a God of justice but some people in authority on the earth have allowed satan to enter their hearts and cause them to pervert justice especially for the poor. These people that do such things are not of God and if left to their evil ways, many who do not have a voice will be silenced and mistreated.

God is calling His people to rise up, speak out and take action against governments, people in authority and all those who would use bribery and underhanded means to suppress, depress and silence those who are unable to represent themselves. God is watching and He will not allow injustice to reign in the earth forever.

Chapter 1

SPIRITUAL ATMOSPHERE CHANGING

I am Apostle Marguerite Breedy-Haynes and this is the second part of The Law and broken judicial System In Barbados book.

I must say that it's a small beautiful island but the experience and what I know that goes on in this country is beyond human comprehension. It is a place where if you do not know God you will end up in prison. If God is not with you, those that do not know Him will literally put you in prison. The judicial system in this country is broken and there are a lot of people who would take bribes to put you in prison if you do not have a relationship with the lord Jesus Christ.

If you read the first book about the law and broken judicial system in Barbados, you will understand what I went through. We are in 2024 and I can see that if you as a child of God do not get it together, this country and those who lead this country, will allow you not to have a say in this country. As a pastor who is called to bring the word of God, I began to see a change in this country in 2021 and I knew that God was showing me something that would soon take place in this country such as a dictatorship and the godless nation this country would become.

I was driving with my son one day in the early part of 2021 and I had a sticker on my car which said, "God is Great" when I heard a police siren behind me but I continued on since

I knew that I didn't break any law while driving and I was taking my son to Community College. The police car was driving faster and faster and my son told me to stop.

As I put on my indicator and stopped, these policemen came out of the car and asked me if I had permission to place the sign about God on my car and I said, "no, I don't need permission." The policeman went as far as to tell me to come out of the car but I never came out of the car, instead I was firm with him because I knew that I didn't do anything wrong.

I knew there and then that the climate of Barbados would soon change because there was no good reason why I was being pulled over for a sticker about the lord Jesus on my car. The officer then proceeded to tell me that I should have permission from the government to put a sticker about God on my car.

The sticker was not hiding the number plate infact it was not hiding anything, yet he went so far as to ask to see my license. When he realized that my insurance and everything was paid, he then told me that he would arrest me and I asked him why he would arrest me and I knew that the spiritual climate of the nation was changing. God will allow things to happen to us to let us know where we are in the history of a nation.

I knew that this nation and people were about to go through a tough time because there was a changing of the guards and this time around it was that there was a new party

elected and because of this new party in this island I knew that they would try to get God out of existence in this island.

When I drove off afterwards to continue to take my son

to college, the image in my mind was that I am up for some great persecution and because of this horrible thing that took place in the morning, I realized that my life was in danger. When the spiritual climate of a nation has changed, it means that the godly authority that is supposed to be the nation literally goes away.

When the Barbados Labour Party came in power I didn't feel that God was going to be part of that party because of my previous vision where the Lord told me that there would be a dictatorship coming in. As I watched on and listened I realized that the Barbadian people had made a very big mistake and the nation was going to be godless.

It is important as a people as we go forward, that we do not get tied in to the godless practice of leaders or political leaders but we must continue to look to the Lord in this end time.

Chapter 2

A NATION OF HYPOCRISY

I have been living in this nation Barbados for so long that I can literally tell you the spiritual climate of this nation. It's a nation of hypocrisy and it's a nation that God wants to use but God can never use a nation that never speaks the truth about things that happen there.

Barbados use to be the epicenter of the slave trade and I still believe that many of the people in this country have not come to that place of freedom. I had the opportunity to work among Barbadians and I can say to you that not all, but some of them will betray you in the blink of an eye.

Those who know God will know that they must live according to the rules of God and if God must use this country hypocrisy must not be a part of it. Even in the Christian society hypocrisy rules but the true nature and the true spirit of God cannot overtake the nation because of hypocrisy. The judicial system is wrecked, the church is wrecked and hypocrisy controls the nation, the people and the atmosphere.

God almighty has not been able to take full access because it is the hardest ground for revival. There is such a fear and control in this country that I believe if the people of God who worship Him in spirit and truth do not rise up- from what the lord almighty has shown me- I believe the country will become like communist China (where many Chinese do not have rights).

As I worked in many parts of Barbados there were things that happened and they refused to speak and refused to give an account of what has taken place with others. It is important to understand that God will judge us for not standing up for the rights of those that cannot stand up for themselves.

I have heard the reports of many things that have taken place with poor people in this judicial system and they never had the chance to be able to exercise their rights. This is because they are poor and this country is a country of who knows who. Those who know others are able to get away with murder and even policemen are able to get away with drugs, yet a poor person is pushed down and put in prison forever.

When this country begins to understand that God watches and he looks down from heaven and sees everything, then there should be equal rights given for all mankind and a lot of things would be different. I pray that the judicial system in this country will become one where people have the right to be able to stand up for themselves.

I had an opportunity to visit the prison here in Barbados and my heart broke. Why did my heart break into pieces? It was because I saw young men that could have received the necessary help in order to do better but they couldn't because they did not receive the help. The broken judicial system in this country is something to think about and I think that human rights activists must look into what is going on here in the prison system of Barbados.

What can the government do to be able to help young men? Maybe these young men have murdered someone because of the type of society they grew up in or what has taken place in their homes. I really think that the system of Barbados is not there to help you but to break you.

My greatest desire as I continue to live in this nation is to see that those who need help get the necessary help that they need by calling upon the name of the Lord. Instead we see systems that are being put in place to destroy the nation or the people of the nation instead of building them up.

We need spiritual and political leaders that will help to create an environment to uplift people rather than themselves. When we see the life of Jesus, He did not try to uplift Himself but everything was about the will of the Father. We are living in a world that is selfish and individuals that take the highest post in the land become self-centered instead of taking care of the people of the land, so there is a lot of neglect instead of helping others to become better.

This book is written to help those that will read it to give their lives as vessels of honor to benefit the nations instead of themselves.

Chapter 3

NO TRUE JUSTICE FOR THE POOR

Just recently there was something on the news about a minister of the government's child who had one of those diplomatic passports and she was able to leave one nation to come to Barbados with illegal drugs. When she arrived here, the authorities informed the Barbadian public about what she did yet by the next day the young woman was seen on the road. My concern is that if it was another person who didn't have diplomatic immunity they would have been lost away in prison

Is there favoritism in our nation? Another person would have never seen the light of day. There is no true justice for the poor in Barbados, it is about who you know and who has the clout. I believe that God is looking down and seeing the injustice taking place and if punishment is being given out, it should go to all people the same way. Not thinking that one person is better than another. True justice must be the same for all people, not having justice just because you have some sort of favor from an individual.

There was another case where a policeman was held with a lot of drugs and up until today, we have not heard anything about that case or what happened to that officer. God almighty is looking at all of those things that are happening in Barbados. I have lived here for a very long time, and I have seen the injustice that goes on in the lives of people and how some people are treated better than others. The justice system in rigged and there is no true justice for the poor.

I believe the lord God almighty is looking down and seeing the injustice that is being done to the poor and I believe that one day he will deal with such things. The nation is all about favoritism such as who you know and who is your godfather and there are a lot of things that are being swept under the carpet. It's a nation of lies and hypocrisy and it's a nation that does not really speak about the wrong that is being done.

I believe that this is because of the nature of the slave, as this country was the slave epicenter for the entire Caribbean. The people are not free and even within this new administration they are trying to subdue the people. My prayer is that many would understand that now is the time to stand up and talk about the rigged judicial system in this country.

It is so rigged that even the civil servants in this country cannot really speak. There is no justice for them. How can a person be part of the civil service in a nation and when something is happening to you, you can't speak to defend yourself? Freedom of speech is not allowed for the people, not even the ability to voice your concerns on the radio. Everything is hidden and thrown under the carpet but God almighty will deal with this at some point.

Chapter 4

MURDERS IN POLICE STATIONS

One of the things about Barbados is that it's a beautiful country. It's a country that anyone around the world would love and it is a very relaxing place to travel to. However, there are a lot of hidden agendas that takes place in the country. For instance, there has been a few deaths that have taken place in police custody and the right authorities would not even check to see how these young men were killed.

There are mothers in this nation that are really crying out and speaking out about this because they know that their children lost their lives in police custody. There are even witnesses who have seen young men lose their life in prison being murdered in the cell.

The justice system is so rigged in this country that if someone dies in police custody, what the police say is what they would go with. I think we need to have greater forensic scientists in this country to find out how someone died in police custody.

The time has come for the justice system in Barbados to care about the lives of the people and regardless of if somebody committed a murder, we need to care about what goes on in this country. This country is too small for the level of things that goes on here but it looks like people don't want to speak about it but sweep it underneath the carpet.

I have had many people that came to me who work in police stations that have witnessed murders in the cells and when people come in to work they say to them, "unfortunately this person has just died." Without any true or good investigation as to what happened to that individual.

I believe the authorities of this country have a lot to answer God for and the blood of these men, regardless of if they are criminals or not, is crying out in this country and it is time for true justice to take place.

A young man may have ended up in court for shooting someone but there are cops in this island that are literal murderers that need to be dealt with as well. The justice system in this country is so rigged that lives does not matter to those that don't have anyone to answer to.

I have found that when someone commits a murder here, after they get to a police station, their lives are at stake. I believe that the lord Jesus is looking at some of the things that are going on here. When I was arrested here in Barbados I felt that if God was not with me, I would have become a statistic.

I did not murder anybody nor did I do anything like what some of these young men have done, yet the way I was treated by some of the police women told me that they have the ability to murder people.

I am not saying that all policemen are like this but I am telling you what I observed and have seen here in this country.

The time will come when God will bring wrong things right in this country because the blood of the innocent is crying out from the hands of some policemen in this country.

It's time to reflect and as the good book says, "God's eyes go to and fro in the earth." If the justice system of Barbados does not get itself together and the people realize what really takes place in this country, I believe we will see the hands of God, just like how Cain killed Abel and God put a mark on him so that no one would touch him.

Remember that I am not saying that someone should not pay for something they have done, but when we start to murder people and no one is speaking up about it, that is wrong. I have evidence of young men that have been murdered and up until now mothers cannot find out who has murdered their children and this is wrong.

The justice system in Barbados needs to be looked after. I believe that human rights activists need to see what is going on in the prison system and also what is happening to people that are in police custody here in Barbados.

Chapter 5

SPIRITUAL CONDITION DEAD

For a long time, Barbados has been on a downward spiral in a spiritual way. Many Barbadians have allowed things like Crop Over and other festive times to take over the spiritual climate of the nation. It's a very religious country but I believe for Barbados to become what God wants it to become, the nation will have to go through some really dangerous times.

Everybody's talking about revival but revival never happens until disaster comes. This nation needs to come to a place where they have to suffer for God. In my dreams the Lord showed me great persecution that will come to this country with pastors being arrested and we are heading there.

If we do not understand that God is calling us to a different and higher place, we will never be able to reach where he wants us to be. Barbados is one of the hardest grounds for the gospel of Jesus Christ and if you are not strong, you will literally fall through the cracks.

I have come to realize that the reason why the spiritual condition of this nation is dead is because you cannot mix God with the devil. There are many pastors in this country that have joined the masonic lodge and there are many pastors that are part of the demonic realm in this country.

We need to decide either to serve God or the devil because a nation cannot thrive in God until that nation understands that God is the only one that can make us live and thrive. As a pastor, if I was not in God, I am telling you I would not survive because some of the people are very cold.

As a pastor if you're not careful, you will not make it as a spiritual leader in this country. Again I say to you that it is time for revival to come but revival will not come unless disaster comes. God must bring the people into a place of the testing of time because when we are tested we will be able to call upon the name of the Lord. Calling on God especially during testing times is what will cause us to have a deeper relationship with the lord Jesus Christ.

I watched closely during the election time of Barbados and I began to see the people deviate or remove themselves from the path of God. There was more than one political party, yet the people here in this country knew exactly who they would vote for. Instead of choosing one that is moral, they chose the immoral. They did not choose one that would stand up for the values and things of God in this country.

Even Christians campaigned for the immoral and when we look at things like that and the devaluing of marriage values such as male with female, all of these things show us that the spiritual leaders here can't see certain things. It also tells you that God is not existence in the lives of these people and these people are just playing games with the Lord.

For Barbados to really excel in the spirit and in whatever God has called the nation to excel in, I believe we have to come to a place of no compromise. We need to go back to the values that the founding fathers of this nation thrived on. Until we realize this, the nation will continue to sink in a hole.

It is my duty to make sure that everyone who reads this book begins to understand that God is calling us all back to His values that this nation was founded on.

Chapter 6

GREAT FEAR IN THE NATION

There is a powerful scripture in the book of Samuel where Samuel was a leader of Israel and a mighty prophet of God and at that time, God had given people himself as ruler but they didn't want him. They wanted something that they thought was better than God. We can take a lesson from the children of Israel who had God as their leader but ended up making a bad decision.

Sometimes we look at all the other nations and want things the same way as them but we don't know what we are asking for. In that day, the people didn't want Samuel as their leader anymore and Samuel cried out to God and God told him to let them have what they wanted. God was saying, if they wanted to put him aside or discard him, he would let them do so.

Samuel allowed the people to choose the king and put God aside, but after that, the Lord said that those who put him aside will face the penalty or the suffering that needs to come. The king that they chose was king Saul. This is what Barbados did, they removed one man that they said was not speaking and was silent or mute and they put a woman that to them was charismatic.

They knew exactly who she was but they put this woman that was charismatic in, a woman that did not know God, who suddenly started to put laws in place which meant that the people couldn't talk anymore, not even the news media could talk. Why? It is because when she came in power, she silenced the mouths of the people.

The fact is that when we choose other gods above the almighty God, He will let us have what we want to have but there will be consequences that follow. As I look at Barbados, I see a nation that is going through a terrible transition and if those of us that hear do not take note, I believe that we will not be able to have freedom of speech at all.

This lady that is in power is not only a dictator but she's a tyrant and she really doesn't care about the views of the people. She's narcissistic! Barbadians must rise up and they must understand that because we have put God out and put this individual in, if we are not careful and return to God while there is still time, we will suffer greater consequences than we have ever thought of in our lifetime.

Chapter 7

BRIBERY

I remember one time the lord showing me some things that would take place in that nation of Barbados. I had a dream where I was at the airport and I had the privilege of seeing some sort of terrorists coming into the country. When they came in I saw a transaction that was going on between immigration officers and these terrorists. I saw an exchange of money.

Bribery is one of the things that will stop us from being loyal to our nation and it is something that stops us from being committed to the work that we are called to do. As a people if we like to take bribes, it means that the justice system in Barbados will not be all that it's supposed to be because we are not working the way that God has truly called us to work.

I remember I had a dream that there was a franchise chain taking over from KFC in Barbados and in this dream the Lord was showing me how they were able to build many of these franchises through money laundering. Yet the Barbadian politicians are suppressing many of the people here in Barbados.

These people would love to make money online but they cannot because the suppression that comes to the poor people of this nation is beyond human comprehension. Imagine that God showed me that this franchise that is all over Barbados is operated by money laundering and poor people are not able to get through.

What I want to speak about today is that the justice system in Barbados is rigged beyond what you can think about and the poor people in the country are being suppressed. There are those in Barbados who have talent but they cannot use that talent. They cannot even make money on you tube and many other places because the system is rigged and set up to make you poor. However, the big McGuffey's in Barbados are able to launder money and build franchises.

Barbados is such a beautiful country and it has so much potential, yet big McGuffey's are suppressing those who want to make themselves better. The justice system of Barbados is set up to make you fail in this life but I believe that the almighty God will deal with this at some point in life. The Lord will deal with this matter.

Bribery is something else, they put laws in place for the poor but not for the middle class and those that are filthy rich in Barbados and this is so sad in this time and season. For us to be able to remove ourselves from being poor in this country, the government must look at what is taking place because they are the ones who put the systems in place that stop even the young people from making money.

How on earth is this franchise that has taken over Barbados able to make lots of money to build more franchises, yet they are not getting their money the right way? The government says that they need to put things in place for money laundering yet the Lord Jesus showed me this franchise here in Barbados is doing that very thing.

You see, the poor becomes poorer and the rich becomes richer. These same people are using methods of bribery and doing other under handed things while the poor here in Barbados are not able to do anything. It is my duty as a child of God to really pray for this country because this country and its system is rigged.

Chapter 8

WHO KNOWS WHO

I have been living in this country for many years from a child and the operation of this country is just something else, the rich becomes richer and the poor becomes poorer. It is a system of not only money laundering that passes between the rich but it's a system of who knows who.

The fact is that if you have to live in this country and be able to reach to your highest potential, you have to understand that you need to know God or you will not make it. As I walk the streets of Barbados, I can see the young men on the block and the depressed behavioral pattern that they are displaying each day.

These young men do not have a godfather to be able to remove them from the heavy Babylonian system that is in this country. If you do not have a relationship with Jesus Christ, a true relationship and know how to press forward, you will not be able to make it in this land because who knows who, is who gets through.

I remember at one time I was working at a government facility in this country and every time I was sent to get a permanent job another person came in front of me and at that time, I was depressed. However, I believe what was meant for evil, God turns it around for the good. I also believe that the Lord did not really want me in the government system of this country because of what He had called me to do.

This country is all about who knows who and if you know somebody or somebody knows somebody, and if you are at a high level you will get where you're supposed to go. Just recently there was a policeman that was a lawyer in this country who was involved with a system of drugs and he was held, yet we never heard anything about that case, that case was just thrown through the back door.

It was just a stroll through the backdoor for him but if that had been my son or someone else's son who does not know somebody high up in this country, they would have gone straight to jail. My friend, God almighty is watching the unfairness that is going on in this island and what is happening to the people, just like the lord sent the angels to Abraham to say He had seen the suffering of His people in Egypt.

Barbados is like a type of Egypt or colonial Babylon where the system says that if you if you do not know somebody
in this country you will not be able to make it in this lifetime. I am calling on you as I'm writing this book with

confidence allowing you to know that it is time for you and I as children of God to stand up for your right.

Like Bob Marley sang, "get up, stand up, stand up for you're right." This is a controlling system, a system where you really cannot express yourself and if you're not bold enough you will not make it through. I need you to hear me out and break through the iron curtain, and put your head above the waters so that you can reach should greet us heights in God.

Chapter 9

THOSE IN AUTHORITY NEVER PAY THE FULL PRICE FOR THEIR CRIMES

What type of country is this country? It's a country where those that are in authority never pay the full price for the crime that they commit. It is a country that is made up to destroy the innocent, the poor and those that people think cannot stand up for themselves. That is why I say to you that the justice system of this country is rigged.

The people that are in a high position never pay the full price for their crimes. Barbados is a country that says that they put things in place but many of the laws that are put in place in this country are laws that destroy the innocent and poor.

We have this present administration that is in power and

from the time they came in power, there was no jobs for the poor unprivileged people instead there were laws that were put in place to destroy the innocent in this land. The government system in this country is just beyond human comprehension.

How on earth during covid-19 time was there a law put in place for a fifty thousand dollars fine for those who disobeyed the government? I want all Barbadians to open their eyes, understand what is taking place and want better for themselves and their children because the system of government that is in this country is only placed to destroy the people of the land instead of elevating them.

Look at the governmental systems that we put in power, are they truly for the people or are they only for what benefits them, their children and those that are on the same level as them? We truly need to look at this! During covid-19, there were those in authority who allowed their children to go outside by giving them passes, yet the people who voted for this administration couldn't go out. They even had passes where they could do transactions but the normal people could not.

What is this? Are we living in a communist nation? When I look at what was taking place, I realized that they were setting up a system to bring people to their knees. Although all of this has taken place, Barbadians have not yet realized that this present administration is not for them.

I am a living testimony as to what took place during covid-19. During this time, I saw that when the people were about to go to the shops, they had to go to do so by their surname. I said to myself that this was not right because God does not treat us this way but this nation could not understand what God was trying to show them.

The lord was trying to show the nation something that is about to come but the people thought it was just a disease and that they had to follow the protocol that was given. It is time for us to wake up and challenge the system in this country or else we will not live long and our children will suffer in time to come.

Chapter 10

THERE IS NO TRUE JUSTICE

A couple of years ago I had a powerful and vivid vision that could not be ignored and that is what caused me to realize that many of those working in government in Barbados are people who take bribes. They will not live for righteousness. It is a broken system that will take bribes instead of doing what is right and as the Bible tells us, a righteous man is one who will stand up for the cause of the poor. They will even stand up for their own country and not take bribes.

Just recently there was some allegations against a homeless man that they claimed went into parliament and stole some artefacts from the building but this man has been disoriented for many years. What we need to know is who it is that really broke into parliament!

There is no true justice. How can you arrest a homeless man that has been disorientated or mad (crazy) for many years thinking that he can break into the protected parliament building and just pick up artefacts? The fact is that they just wanted somebody to punish and take the fall for what had taken place.

At this very moment no one in Barbados is really speaking up, this injustice happened because this man does not have a voice. It doesn't matter whether you are poor or whether you are rich, I believe that everybody should be judged equally

and according to what they have done. However, this man by the name of **ninja man** did not do these things and many Barbadians know this.

Why is the public so quiet? It is because there is no true justice in a land of compromise, a land that sweeps things under the carpet. A land that puts falsehood in front of truth. I truly believe that God will bring justice to the poor just like He did before when Israel cried out in Egypt.

I believe that there is an Egyptian or Babylonian rule that governs this country and our lawmakers must understand that there needs to be true justice. But whether or not there is true justice in Barbados or not, there is true justice in the heavens and God will bring justice to those who cry to him in the night.

Just like the woman who kept pursuing the unjust judge for justice, God is going to bring justice to those who need justice. This woman in the bible was not receiving justice, but as she wore out that judge, she received it and we need to wear out the government with cries for justice. Those of you who are reading this book, I need you to rise up!

They have always said that Barbados is one of the most peaceful countries but is it truly peaceful or is it a country of hypocrisy? Is it peaceful or is it a country that is still under heavy slavery? Barbados used to be the epicenter for the slave trade and even though many are educated and think that this is one of the most educated places in the Caribbean, the people are still mentally, physically, and emotionally under slavery because they don't have the right to truly speak for what they believe.

This is a time and a season for Barbadians to have a revolutionary mind and way of thinking of a better future. In order to be better, we must stand up for what we believe and we must stand up for what is not lawful in this land. I believe there should be equal rights for all men because when there are not equal rights it means that we are putting another person above ourselves that really does not deserve to be there.

There is something that I know for sure that comes with being police officers, nurses and those who receive promotions in government in this country. It is that the masonic lodge rules and many have received promotions because of their affiliation with such institutions.

This is not right. People have even been let out from prison because of such affiliation. I believe that in order for this country to get to the place were God wants it to be, Christians will have to really pray because we are fighting against an evil force in all of the sectors here in this country.

Appreciation

I would like to extend a very heartfelt thank you, first to God the Father, Son and Holy Spirit who directed me in writing this book. To my immediate family for their constant support. To Apostle Anthony Greaves, Miss. Valarie Deane, Allan Isaac and Prophetess Debbie Isaac who saw the anointing upon my life when no one else saw it.

I am very grateful to Pastor Cheryl Harewood for believing in my calling and I would like to extend my sincerest gratitude to Anthony Devonish, Reverend Michelle Marshall, Reverend Wasim Worrell, Reverend Kerrie Worrell, Reverend Waldron, Minister Waldron, Evangelist Arlene, Minister Maria Clarke and the members of the congregation for standing with me in ministry.

About The Author

Apostle Marguerite Breedy-Haynes was born in St. Lucia to one Barbadian parent and one St. Lucian parent and is the seventh of sixteen children. She lived in Barbados since childhood and has three children.

Saved by Jesus who visited her in a vision, she was taken to hell, and there she was given a mandate by God not to let anyone go to that place. She then gave her life completely over to Him and was anointed as an End Time Prophet. Her ministry began by giving tracts on the streets of Barbados for over 3 years until God promoted her.

Saving The Lost At Any Cost, End Time Ministries' was started at her house and has now become an international ministry with branches based in Barbados, South Carolina, St. Lucia and several others which are being birthed around the world. Hundreds came to her from all over Barbados. Their lives were changed through the deliverance of the Word of God, many were healed and demons were cast out.

As an End Time Prophet, she was called to preach the gospel of the second coming of the Lord Jesus Christ. She has travelled the world ministering in various churches and crusades, teaching and admonishing others to live holy lives before God. She is known for not compromising the Word of God and believes in living what she preaches. Her desire is to win souls for the end times and to snatch God's children from the hands of the enemy.

I pray that this book has been a blessing to you. For more information on the author, her ministry and her books, please contact us or visit us at:

Telephone: (246) 249-3265/622-2301

Website:
https://margueritebreedyhaynesministriesinternational.com

Address: Saving The Lost At Any Cost End Time Ministries

The Old Montgomery Boys School
Cave Hill
St. Michael

Facebook:
https://www.facebook.com/savingthelostinternational/

Twitter: https://twitter.com/savingthelost1

Medium: https://medium.com/@savingthelost

Email: savingthelost@live.com

Instagram: Savingthelostatanycost

Journal

www.ingramcontent.com/pod-product-compliance
Lightning Source LLC
Chambersburg PA
CBHW070215260726
48658CB00006BA/2087